PHINEAS GAGE
A Gruesome but True Story
About Brain Science

PHINEAS GAGE

A Gruesome but True Story About Brain Science

by JOHN FLEISCHMAN

 Houghton Mifflin Company *Boston*

www.houghtonmifflinbooks.com

Book design by Lisa Diercks
The text of this book is set in Janson Text.

Library of Congress Cataloging-in-Publication Data
    Fleischman, John.
    Phineas Gage: a gruesome but true story about brain science / by John Fleischman
        p. cm.
    RNF ISBN 0-618-05252-6 PAP ISBN 0-618-49478-2
    1. Gage, Phineas — Mental health. 2. Brain damage — Patients — United States —
Biography. 3. Brain damage — Complications. 4. Personality disorders — Etiology. I. Title.
    RC387.5 .F565 2002
    362.1'97481044'092—dc21
    [B]   2001039253

Printed in Singapore
TWP 20 19 18 17 16 15 14

As always, for Mary

Acknowledgments

To Tim Clark, who gave me the time and place to begin. To my medical readers, Dr. Robert Pressberg, Dr. Barbara Skolnick, and Dr. Jeffrey Macklis, who are responsible only for correct anatomical facts, the author being responsible for all errors. To Virginia Hunt of the Countway Library of Medicine, Harvard Medical School, who was so generally helpful. To Dr. Denise Natale of the Cavendish Chamber of Commerce, who never lost patience with Phineas. To Dr. Joseph Gall and the American Society for Cell Biology for Hooke's flea and Hooke's cells. To Dr. Malcolm Macmillan of Deakin University, Australia, who knows more than anyone about Phineas Gage, and to Amy Flynn, who did not blanch at first glance.

PHINEAS GAGE
A Gruesome but True Story
About Brain Science

"Horrible Accident" in Vermont

The most unlucky/lucky moment in the life of Phineas Gage is only a minute or two away. It's almost four-thirty in the afternoon on September 13, 1848. Phineas is the foreman of a track construction gang that is in the process of blasting a railroad right-of-way through granite bedrock near the small town of Cavendish, Vermont. Phineas is twenty-six years old, unmarried, and five feet, six inches tall, short for our time but about average for his. He is good with his hands and good with his men, "possessing an iron will as well as an iron frame," according to his doctor. In a moment, Phineas will have a horrible accident.

It will kill him, but it will take another eleven years, six months, and nineteen days to do so. In the short run, Phineas will make a full recovery, or so it will seem to those who didn't know him before. Old friends and family will know the truth. Phineas will never be his old self again. His "character" will change. The ways in which he deals with others, conducts himself, and makes plans will all change. Long after the accident, his doctor will sum up his case for a medical journal. "Gage," his doctor will write, "was no longer Gage." Phineas Gage's accident will make him world famous, but fame will do him little good. Yet for many others—psychologists, medical researchers, doctors, and especially those who suffer brain injuries—Phineas Gage will become someone worth knowing.

That's why we know so much about Phineas. It's been 150 years since his accident, yet we are still learning more about him. There's also a lot about Phineas we don't know and probably never will. The biggest question is the simplest one and the hardest to answer: Was Phineas lucky or unlucky? Once you hear his story, you can decide for yourself. But right now, Phineas is working on the railroad and his time has nearly come.

Building a railroad in 1848 is muscle work. There are no bulldozers or power shovels to open a way through Vermont's Green Mountains for the Rutland & Burlington Railroad. Phineas's men work with picks, shovels, and rock drills. Phineas's special skill is blasting. With well-placed charges of black gunpowder, he shatters rock. To set those charges, he carries the special tool of the blasting trade, his "tamping iron." Some people confuse a tamping iron with a crowbar, but they are different tools for different jobs. A crowbar is for lifting up or prying apart something heavy. A tamping iron is for the delicate job of setting explosives. Phineas had his tamping iron made to order by a neighborhood blacksmith. It's a tapering iron rod that is three feet, seven inches long and weighs thirteen and a half pounds. It looks like an iron spear. At the base, it's fat and round, an inch and three quarters in diameter. The fat end is for tamping—packing down—loose powder. The other end comes to a sharp, narrow point and is for poking holes through the gunpowder to set the fuse. Phineas's tamping iron is very smooth to the touch, smooth from the blacksmith's forge as well as from constant use.

His task is to blast the solid rock into pieces small enough for his crew to dig loose with hand tools and haul away in ox carts. The first step is to drill a hole in the bedrock at exactly the right angle and depth, or the explosion will be wasted. All day, Phineas must keep an eye on his drillers to make sure they stay ahead. All day, Phineas must keep an eye on his diggers to make sure they keep up. All the time between, Phineas and his assistant are working with touchy explosives.

They follow a strict routine. His assistant "charges" each new hole by filling the bottom with coarse-grained gunpowder. Phineas uses the narrow end of his iron to carefully press the ropelike fuse down into the powder. The assistant then fills up the rest of the hole with loose sand to act as a plug. Phineas will tamp the sand tight to bottle up the explosion, channeling the blast downward into the rock to shatter it. While his assistant is pouring the sand, Phineas flips his tamping iron around from the pointy end to the round end for tamping. Black powder is ticklish stuff. When it's damp, nothing will set it off.

When it's too dry or mixed in the wrong formula, almost anything can set it off, without warning. But Phineas and his assistant have done this a thousand times—pour the powder, set the fuse, pour the sand, tamp the sand plug, shout a warning, light the fuse, and run like mad.

But something goes wrong this time. The sand is never poured down the hole; the black powder and fuse sit exposed at the bottom. Does his assistant forget, or does Phineas forget to look? Witnesses disagree. A few yards behind Phineas, a group of his men are using a hand-cranked derrick crane to hoist a large piece of rock. Some of the men remember seeing Phineas standing over the blast hole, leaning lightly on the tamping iron. Others say Phineas was sitting on a rock ledge above the hole, holding the iron loosely between his knees.

There is no argument about what happens next. Something or someone distracts Phineas. Does he hear his name called? Does he spot someone goofing off? Whatever the reason, Phineas turns his head to glance over his right shoulder. The fat end of his tamping iron slips down into the hole and strikes the granite. A spark flies onto the exposed blasting powder. Blam! The drill hole acts as a gun barrel. Instead of a bullet, it fires Phineas's rod straight upward. The iron shrieks through the air and comes down with a loud clang about thirty feet away.

This is what happens. Imagine you are inside Phineas's head, watching in

This is the face of the man with a hole in his head. It's a plaster life mask of Phineas Gage made in Boston after his accident, and it shows exactly what the "recovered" Phineas looked like a year after his accident. He was twenty-seven. Notice the big scar on his forehead. To see what lies beneath the scar, compare this to the picture of his skull on page 62. *Photograph by Doug Mindell; life mask courtesy of the Warren Anatomical Museum, Countway Library of Medicine, Harvard Medical School*

extreme slow motion: See the pointy end of the rod enter under his left cheekbone, pass behind his left eye, through the front of his brain, and out the middle of his forehead just above the hairline. It takes a fraction of a fraction of a second for the iron rod to pass from cheekbone to forehead, through and through.

Amazingly, Phineas is still alive. The iron throws him flat on his back, but as his men come running through the gunpowder smoke, he sits up. A minute later, he speaks. Blood is pouring down his face from his forehead, but Phineas is talking about the explosion. His men insist on carrying him to an ox cart for the short ride into town. They gently lift him into the back of the cart so he can sit up with his legs out before him on the floor. An Irish workman grabs a horse and races ahead for the doctor while the ox cart ambulance rumbles slowly down the half-mile to Cavendish. Phineas's excited men crowd alongside, walking next to their injured boss. Still acting as a foreman, Phineas calls out for his time book and makes an entry as he rolls toward town.

Something terrible has happened, yet Phineas gets down from the cart without help. He climbs the steps of the Cavendish hotel, where he has been living, and takes a seat on the porch beside his landlord, Joseph Adams. A few minutes earlier, Adams had seen the Irishman ride past shouting for Dr. Harlow, the town physician. Dr. Harlow was not to be found, so the rider was sent

---

Lucky or unlucky, the sharp angle of the tamping iron made all the difference to Phineas. It entered just under his left cheekbone, passed behind his left eyeball, and continued on upward through his frontal lobes. It exited his forehead between the two hemispheres of the cortex. The iron's passage left him alive and conscious but forever changed. *Illustration by Jerry Malone*

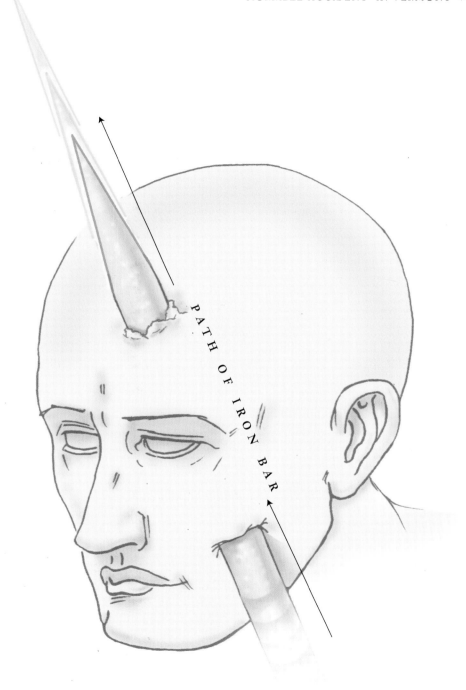

PATH OF IRON BAR

on to the next village to fetch Dr. Williams. Now Phineas takes a neighborly seat on the porch and tells his landlord what happened to him.

That's how Dr. Edward Williams finds Phineas nearly thirty minutes after the accident. Dr. Williams pulls up in his buggy at the hotel porch, and there is Phineas, talking away. Friends, workmates, and the curious crowd around as Dr. Williams climbs down from his carriage. "Well, here's work enough for you, Doctor," Phineas says to him quite cheerfully.

Dr. Williams examines Phineas's head. He can't believe that this man is still alive. His skull is cracked open, as if something has popped out from the inside. Accident victims are often too shaken to know what happened, so Dr. Williams turns to Phineas's workmen for the story, but Phineas insists on speaking for himself. He tells Dr. Williams that the iron went right through his head.

Dr. Williams does not believe him. "I thought he was deceived," Dr. Williams writes in his notes. "I asked him where the bar entered, and he pointed to the wound on his cheek, which I had not before discovered. This was a slit running from the angle of the jaw forward about one and a half inch. It was very much stretched laterally, and was discolored by powder and iron rust, at least appeared so. Mr. Gage persisted in saying that the bar went through his head. An Irishman standing by said, 'Sure it was so, sir, for the bar is lying in the road below, all blood and brains.'"

It's now an hour after the accident. The town's regular physician, Dr. John Martyn Harlow, finally arrives at the hotel. The two doctors confer, but Dr. Harlow takes over the case. Phineas is a gruesome sight. Bleeding freely from his forehead and inside his mouth, Phineas looks to Dr. Harlow like a wounded man just carried in from a battlefield. Yet Phineas is alert, uncomplaining, and still telling anyone who'll listen about the accident. Dr. Harlow wants Phineas to come in off the porch so he can treat his wound. Phineas gets up and, leaning only lightly on Dr. Harlow's arm, climbs up a long flight of stairs to his room. He lies down on his own bed so Dr. Harlow can shave his head and examine the wound more closely. What the doctor sees is terrible. Something has erupted through the top of Phineas's head, shattering the skull in its path and opening the brain to plain sight.

Dr. Harlow does what he can. He cleans the skin around the hole, extracts the small fragments of bone, and gently presses the larger pieces of skull back in place. He looks inside Phineas's mouth. He can see the hole where the iron passed upward through the roof of his mouth. Dr. Harlow decides to leave the hole open so the wound can drain. Then Dr. Harlow "dresses" the wound, pulling the loose skin back into position and taping it in place with adhesive strips. He puts a compress bandage directly over the wound and pulls Phineas's nightcap down tightly over it. Finally he winds a roller bandage around his forehead to hold all the bandages securely. Only then does he notice Phineas's hands and forearms, which are black with powder burns. Dr. Harlow dresses the burnt skin and has Phineas put to bed with his head elevated. He gives strict orders that his patient is to remain in that position.

Phineas should have been dead long before this. A thirteen-pound iron rod through the head should kill a person instantly. Surviving that, he should have died of shock soon after reaching Cavendish. He's lost a lot of blood, yet he remains awake and talkative. Even surviving the loss of blood, Phineas should have died of brain swelling. Any hard blow to the body causes injured tissue to swell. The brain is soft, and the skull is hard. A hard blow to the head can rattle the brain around inside like a BB in a tin can. The rattling bruises the brain, and bruised tissue swells. The brain swells, but the skull stays the same size; a swollen brain can jam itself so tightly it will cut off its own blood supply. This swelling can choke off oxygen to parts of the brain long enough to cause permanent damage. It can also cause death.

That's a "closed brain" injury (sometimes called a concussion). The possibility of a closed brain injury is why doctors fuss if you bang your head falling off a bicycle or crashing a car or getting hit hard in the head with anything. (To prevent closed brain injuries, you should wear a helmet when bicycling, driving a race car, fighting in the infantry, playing tackle football, parachuting, exploring a cave, working on a construction site, or doing just about anything where you could strike your head hard. In Phineas's case, however, a helmet would not have helped.)

Here Phineas has a stroke of luck. His is an "open brain" injury. The hole on top of his head gives his battered brain swelling room. The bad news is that his brain is open to infection. At first, though, he does remarkably well. The bleeding from his forehead slows and then stops within twenty-four hours. He remains cheerful and tells Dr. Harlow that he "does not care to see his friends, as he shall be at work in a few days." The morning after the accident, however, he is glad to see his mother and uncle when they arrive from New Hampshire. Two days after the accident, he takes a turn for the worse. He develops a fever and begins to have delirious spells. His wound is leaking a foul-smelling liquid, a sure sign of infection. His death seems just a matter of time now.

More than any other organ, the brain is sealed off from the outside world and from the rest of the body. There are many layers of tissue, bone, and skin to keep it protected from the outside, but there's also a "blood-brain barrier" that keeps out many substances circulating in the blood. Oxygen and nutrients can cross the blood-brain barrier, but many dangerous substances like bacteria cannot. With his skull fractured, Phineas's exposed brain is wide open, making him an ideal candidate for a fatal infection. No one in Cavendish in 1848, no scientist in America or Europe, has the slightest notion that bacteria cause infection.

Medical science in 1848 knows very little about bacteria, even though they were first seen through microscopes nearly two hundred years before. Today we are used to seeing the microscopic world, but when the microscope was invented in the middle of the seventeenth century, it caused a sensation. The microscope became a new kind of "high-tech" entertainment for cultured gentlemen, and in 1665 an Englishman named Robert Hooke came up with a microscopic "hit." He showed off a slide he'd made of an extremely thin slice of cork. Under the microscope lens, Hooke saw that the tissue inside a cork tree was made up of rows of tiny, boxlike structures. They reminded him of the bare rooms used by monks in a monastery. Hooke called them "cells." His cork cells, though, were empty because they were dead and dried out. It would take two centuries to figure out that it's the living stuff inside cells that makes them the fundamental unit of life.

While Hooke was showing off his "cells," a sharp-eyed Dutch merchant named Anton van Leeuwenhoek was making more powerful microscopes. Leeuwenhoek took a single drop of water from a rain barrel and turned his microscope on it. In that drop of water, Leeuwenhoek found a whole new planet of very, very small life forms. "Animalcules," he called them. Leeuwenhoek was the first to see single-celled microorganisms, tiny plants and tiny ani-

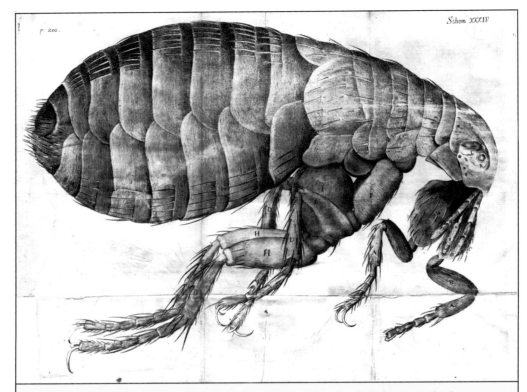

In 1665, the English scientist Robert Hooke published this detailed drawing of a flea as seen through the newly invented microscope. London society clamored to see more microscope images of things too fine for the human eye. *From Hooke's* Micrographica; *courtesy of Dr. Joseph Gall, the Carnegie Institute of Washington, Baltimore, Md.*

mals, including bacteria. Yet Leeuwenhoek never had the faintest suspicion that some of his "animalcules" caused humans to sicken and to die.

That's more or less the state of knowledge in 1848. Few doctors have ever used a microscope, because it is not considered a medical instrument. These microscopic animals might be marvels of nature, but no doctor suspects that they have anything to do with disease, let alone infections. Doctors in 1848 don't use the word *infection*, but they know its symptoms well. They call it "sepsis," and they know from bitter experience how quickly a "septic" wound can go from slight redness to gross swelling to a fatal condition called gangrene.

The doctors of 1848 don't realize that gangrene is the end result of bacterial infection. They don't realize that floating in the air on dust particles, lurking on fingertips, or growing on the shiny steel blades of their unwashed surgical scalpels are single-celled bacteria and other microscopic life forms. On the smallest surface, there are hundreds of millions of them. They represent thousands of different species; there are tiny plants, tiny fungi, tiny viruses, and tiny animals. Among the microanimals are.two particularly dangerous families of bacteria—streptococci and staphylococci ("strep" and "staph," for short). What doctors don't know in 1848, strep and staph do: that the broken head of Phineas is an ideal location to land.

A wound is an open door. A cut or break in the skin lets staph and strep bacteria colonize the warm, wet, nutrient-rich cells inside. Once these bacteria get established in the body, they reproduce wildly. The body's immune system tries to kill the invading bacteria with an array of special immune cells, while the bacteria try to protect themselves against immune cells by cranking out toxic chemicals. That's an infection. The site of this biological battle between the immune system and bacteria swells up and turns red.

In 1848, science is still twenty years away from figuring out that infections are the work of living—that is, "biotic"—things. It will take nearly a century for science to develop the first "antibiotic," penicillin, to counter infections. In 1848, a young Frenchman named Louis Pasteur is still studying chemistry in Paris. Eventually, Pasteur will unravel the three great biological mysteries of

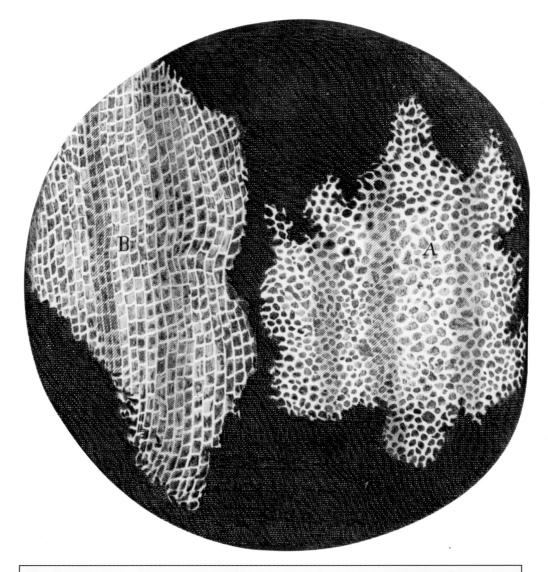

Hooke called the microscopic boxes that he saw in the bark of a cork tree "cells." Compared to his flea pictures, Hooke's cells attracted little notice in 1665. Two centuries later, his "cells" turned out to be the fundamental unit of all life. *From Hooke's* Micrographica; *courtesy of Dr. Joseph Gall, the Carnegie Institute of Washington, Baltimore, Md.*

his time—fermentation, decay, and infection. All three processes are the work of living microorganisms; Pasteur will call them "germs." Pasteur's "germ theory" will lead to a revolution in medicine. It will inspire an English surgeon named Joseph Lister to try performing surgery in sterile conditions that exclude or kill all microorganisms. Lister will scrub his hands almost raw before operating, he will boil surgical clothing and instruments, and he will set up a machine to spray carbolic acid in the operating room to kill germs in midair. Lister's first sterile operations in 1868 will cut the number of deaths from infection after surgery by 90 percent. For the first time in history, doctors will help more patients with surgery than they harm with postsurgical infections.

None of this progress to come will do Phineas a bit of good back in 1848. Instead, Phineas is saved by good luck and good care. Dr. Harlow follows the best medical advice of his time—keep the wound clean but covered and watch for inflammation. A sign of infection is a fluid called "pus" (it's actually dead white blood cells, a sign that the body's immune system is attacking bacterial invaders) that collects in pockets to form abscesses. Fourteen days after the accident, Phineas develops a huge abscess under the skin just above his eyes. Phineas is feverish, losing his appetite, and sinking fast. Dr. Harlow lances (punctures) the abscess. He drains the pus and dresses Phineas's forehead again. The fever abates. His scalp begins to heal. Phineas is saved by his youth, his iron constitution, and Dr. Harlow's good nursing. Dr. Harlow will always be modest about his role in saving Phineas. "I dressed him," Dr. Harlow will say. "God healed him."

The patient gains strength. Too much strength, in his doctor's opinion. Dr. Harlow is called out of town for a few days, and when he comes back he finds

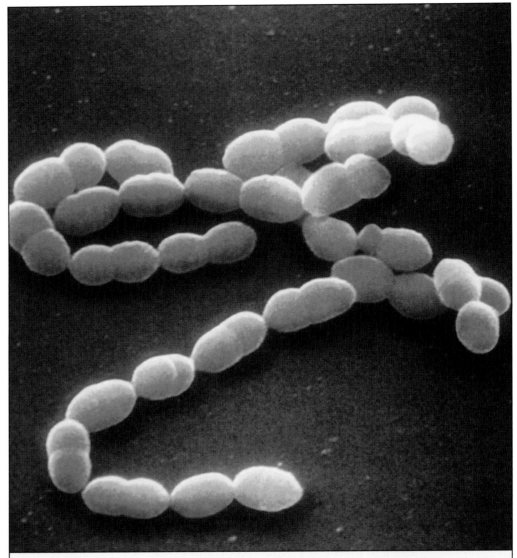

Under the microscope, streptococci bacteria have a distinctive beads-on-a-string appearance. "Strep" bacteria live on nearly everything people touch but are only dangerous if they can penetrate the body's defenses and overpower the immune system. *Microphotograph by H. Morgan, Photo Researchers Inc.*

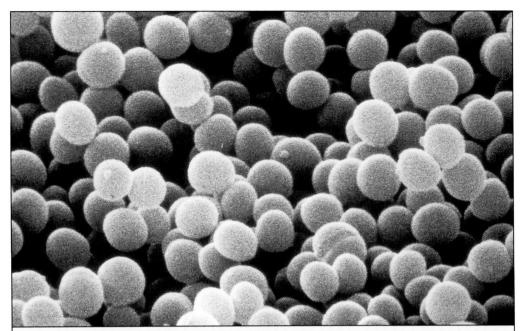

Staphylococci bacteria are the other half of the deadly duo of opportunistic bacteria. Infections by "staph" and "strep" were a leading cause of death before the discovery of antibiotic medicines. Somehow, Phineas's immune system beat off their attack. *Microphotograph by Dr. Tony Brain, Photo Researchers Inc.*

Phineas out of his sickbed. His head still heavily bandaged, Phineas is roaming about Cavendish in the rain with no coat and thin shoes. He is eating unwisely, refusing nursing advice, and ignoring doctor's orders. Phineas says he wants to go home to his mother's house in Lebanon, New Hampshire, twenty miles away. He intends to walk. According to the best medical theories of his day, Dr. Harlow diagnoses an imbalance of bodily "humors." This theory, which goes back to the ancient Greeks, declares that health is maintained by a balance of four liquids, or humors, in the body—blood, phlegm, yellow

bile, and black bile. To bring them into balance, Dr. Harlow prescribes two powerful drugs—an "emetic" to make Phineas throw up and a "purgative," a powerful laxative, to evacuate his bowels. Phineas is knocked flat by the medicines and spends the next two weeks in bed, where Dr. Harlow keeps him on a "low," or bland, diet. His humors may or may not be in balance, but Phineas is resting quietly at last.

Ten weeks after the accident, Dr. Harlow declares Phineas fully recovered from his wounds. He puts Phineas in a closed carriage and sends him home to his mother in New Hampshire. Phineas is very weak, but he can walk short distances. He can count, feed and dress himself, and sing. He can speak clearly and make sense of what he hears. Yet there is something odd about the "recovered" Phineas. Just before he leaves Cavendish, Dr. Harlow gives Phineas a little test. The doctor offers Phineas $1,000 for the pocketful of pebbles that Phineas has collected walking along the Black River near town. Dr. Harlow knows that Phineas can add and subtract, yet Phineas angrily refuses the deal. Dr. Harlow tells himself that a man who was so badly hurt is going to need time to regain his full powers.

As soon as Phineas leaves for home, Dr. Harlow writes a short report for the *Boston Medical & Surgical Journal.* Most doctors ignore Dr. Harlow's article. The few who read it don't believe it. How could a man survive such an

Four hundred years ago, this was an up-to-date medical book illustration. It shows a half-man, half-woman surrounded by the signs of the zodiac and the four "humors" that for centuries doctors believed controlled health—blood, phlegm, black bile, and yellow bile. Balancing the sanguine, or blood, humor was the "reason" for bleeding the sick. *Photo Researchers Inc.*

injury, let alone make a "complete recovery"? But one Boston doctor is intrigued. He writes to Harlow for information and urges the Vermont doctor to back up his case by collecting formal statements from eyewitnesses in Cavendish. The letter is from Henry J. Bigelow, professor of surgery at the Harvard Medical College.

In the spring, Phineas is back in Cavendish, carrying his tamping iron. He never goes anywhere without it these days. Phineas has come for a final examination by Dr. Harlow and to reclaim his old job on the railroad. His left eye looks intact, but the vision has gradually faded away. Phineas has a huge scar on his forehead and a small scar under his cheekbone, but otherwise he is physically healed. Yet Dr. Harlow has private doubts about Phineas's mental state. Phineas is just not his old self.

His old employers on the railroad quickly come to the same conclusion. The new Phineas is unreliable and, at times, downright nasty. He insults old workmates and friends. He spouts vulgar language in the presence of women. He changes his mind and his orders from minute to minute. The railroad contractors let him go. Dr. Harlow, who is keeping confidential notes on Phineas, sadly writes, "His contractors, who regarded him as the most efficient and capable foreman in their employ previous to his injury, considered the change in his mind so marked that they could not give him his place again."

When he was an old man, Dr. Henry J. Bigelow wore a long beard and sober clothes, befitting one of Boston's senior surgeons. But when he was a young man studying medicine in Paris, Bigelow was a snappy dresser. *From a daguerreotype by Leon Foucault, Paris, 1841; courtesy of Countway Library of Medicine, Harvard Medical School*

Phineas's old friends also wash their hands of him. Dr. Harlow writes: "He is fitful, irreverent, indulging at times in the grossest profanity (which was not previously his custom), manifesting but little deference for his fellows, impatient of restraint or advice when it conflicts with his desires." Phineas comes up with all sorts of new plans, the doctor writes, but they are no sooner announced than he drops them. Phineas is like a small child who says he is running away from home after lunch and then comes up with a new idea over his sandwich. Dr. Harlow writes, "A child in his intellectual capacities and manifestations, he has the animal passions of a strong man." A doctor is bound by his oath not to reveal the details of a patient's condition without permission, so Dr. Harlow will keep his observations to himself for twenty years.

Meantime, Dr. Harlow has another letter from Dr. Bigelow at Harvard, who thanks him for collecting the eyewitness statements about the accident. Would Mr. Gage consider coming to Boston at Dr. Bigelow's expense so his case could be presented at the medical school and before the Boston Society of Medical Improvement? Dr. Harlow and Dr. Bigelow make arrangements.

What We Thought
About How We Thought

In the winter of 1850, Phineas goes to Boston so the doctors there can see for themselves. What are doctors like in 1850? They look like gentlemen, or at least they do in the oil portraits that they have painted of themselves to boost their social status. If you lined up a gallery of these doctors' portraits, you'd see a long row of wise faces, satin waistcoats, gold watch chains, and side-whiskers. By 1850, there are photographs of doctors, showing wise faces, satin waistcoats, and whiskers. Photographs of doctors at work, though, are rare. Photographing anyone or anything moving is difficult because the light-sensitive plates are very slow, and a single exposure can take a full minute. Yet the year before Phineas's accident, a Boston photographer named Josiah Hawes sets up his camera in a surgical operating theater and takes a "daguerreotype" (a photograph on a metal plate) that he entitles, "Third Operation Using Ether Anesthesia at the Massachusetts General Hospital." The operating room is called the Ether Dome and still exists today.

The picture that Hawes makes is probably the very first of doctors being doctors instead of doctors posing for portraits. In Hawes's photograph, the surgeons stand impatiently beside the operating table, ready to start work. This is truly a historic moment. Before the introduction of ether a few months before, surgeons had to employ powerful assistants to hold down patients or restrain them with leather-covered chains. Because of the discovery of ether anesthesia, the doctors in the Ether Dome can take their time operating.

Notice two things about Hawes's picture. First, it's all men. There are no female hospital nurses, let alone female doctors. The second thing you should notice is what the doctors are wearing—nothing special. They are in street clothes—black frockcoats, shiny satin vests, and linen shirts. No one is wearing surgical scrubs. No one is wearing surgical gloves, masks, or booties. These doctors may not wash their hands until *after* the operation. These men know nothing about bacteria—but they think they know all about the brain.

This is what an audience of doctors looks like when Phineas arrives in Boston in January 1850, tamping iron in hand. He is Dr. Bigelow's guest but also his prize specimen. Phineas is examined, measured, and discussed. He agrees to sit for a plaster "life" mask. Dr. Bigelow puts straws up Phineas's nose so he can

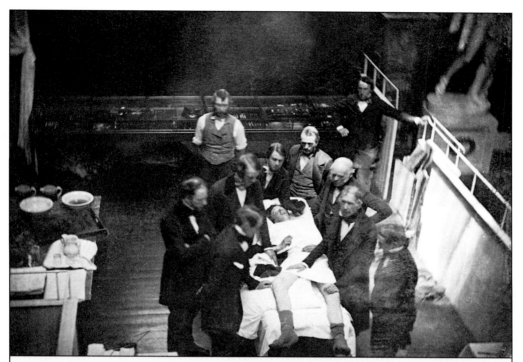

The patient is the one in the cotton gown and wool socks, lying unconscious on the table. Knocked out by inhaling ether fumes, the patient can feel no pain in this state of "twilight sleep." When word of the discovery of anesthesia reached England, a London newspaper rejoiced, announcing, "We Have Conquered Pain." *Massachusetts General Hospital, Archives and Special Collections; print courtesy of Harvard University Art Museums*

breathe while the doctor pours liquid plaster over his face. Then the plaster is lifted off to make a mold. From it, Dr. Bigelow casts a three-dimensional version of Phineas's face. His eyes are shut, but the enormous scar on his forehead is clear.

Phineas appears in person at Dr. Bigelow's lectures to convince the assembled doctors that his case is neither an exaggeration nor a fraud. Dr. Bigelow tackles that question head-on: "The leading feature of this case is its improbability," Dr. Bigelow admits. "A physician who holds in his hand a crowbar, three and a half feet long, and more than thirteen pounds in weight, will not readily believe that it has been driven with a crash through the brain of a man who is still able to walk off, talking with composure and equanimity of the hole in his head. Yet there is every reason for supposing it in this case literally true."

The evidence is standing before them, "crowbar" in hand. Even confronted with that, there are still doctors in the audience who don't believe that the tamping iron went through Phineas's brain. Perhaps, they say, it just hit him a glancing blow on the head. Dr. Bigelow reads out accounts from Dr. Williams and Dr. Harlow. He adds other eyewitness statements from Cavendish people including Mr. Adams, the hotel owner, and some of Phineas's workmen. Dr. Bigelow unveils his plaster life mask of Phineas. The casting clearly shows scars where the iron went in and came out. Yet there are doctors who think that Phineas is a humbug, a fake from the back woods of Vermont.

There are two other groups of doctors paying close attention to Dr. Bigelow's presentation. The two rival groups are eager to believe in Phineas's case. Their theories directly contradict each other, and yet both groups believe that Phineas's case supports their side. As it turns out, both groups are slightly right but mostly wrong. Yet their wrong theories—and Phineas himself—will steer our knowledge of the brain in the right direction.

Everybody knows that people use their brains to think. Right? And, of course, emotions, especially love, come from the heart. Wrong? Obviously, our ideas about how the body works have changed. Three hundred years ago, everybody "knew" that anger was controlled by the spleen. Twenty-three hundred years ago, the ancient Greeks "knew" that the heart was the center of emotion and thought.

Aristotle, the greatest scientist of his time, "knew" that the primary function of the brain was to cool the blood. It isn't until 1800 that an Austrian doctor named Franz Josef Gall declares that the brain is the seat of the intelligence, the emotions, and the will. Still, it takes time for new ideas to sink in. Even today, we don't talk about a lover who's been dumped as feeling "broken-brained."

By Phineas's time, doctors know what a brain looks like, at least from the outside. They learn as students of gross (a term for "large-scale") anatomy by dissecting the cadavers of paupers, prisoners, and the unclaimed. By 1850, all doctors know the gross anatomy of the skeleton, internal organs, muscles, and, of course, the brain. They just don't know how the brain works.

You can have a look for yourself. Imagine you could click open the top of your head and lift your brain out. It weighs about three pounds. Some compare it to half of an enormous walnut, but if you can't visualize a three-pound walnut half, think of a bicycle helmet (bicycle helmets look the way they do so they can surround the brain). Think of your brain as a big cap perched on a stalk and protected by the neck flap. The big cap is your cerebral cortex. The stalk is your brain stem, which plugs into your spinal cord. The brain stem keeps many of your automatic functions going, like your breathing and heartbeat. The neck flap covers your cerebellum, which coordinates movement. Without your cerebellum, you couldn't walk upright, touch your finger to your nose, or turn this page. Without your brain stem, you couldn't breathe. Without your cerebral cortex, you wouldn't be human.

The cortex is where you think, remember, learn, imagine, read, speak, listen, and dream. In the cortex, you feel your emotions and you make sense of what your senses are telling you. The cortex is where you actually see what

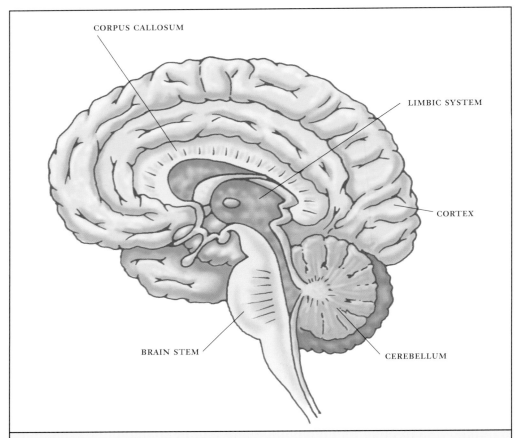

CORPUS CALLOSUM

LIMBIC SYSTEM

CORTEX

BRAIN STEM

CEREBELLUM

This is half a brain. On top and in front is the cortex. In the back and underneath are the cerebellum and the brain stem. On the bottom of the cortex is the limbic system, which coordinates memory, sensation, and emotion. In Phineas's case, the tamping iron passed through the frontal cortex, leaving the rest of his brain relatively unharmed. *Illustration by Jerry Malone*

your eyes transmit, smell what your nose senses, taste what your tongue samples, touch what your nerves report, and hear what your ears pick up. None of this vital activity is visible in gross anatomy. By just holding a brain in your hands you (and the doctors of Phineas's day) can't see the thing that makes this

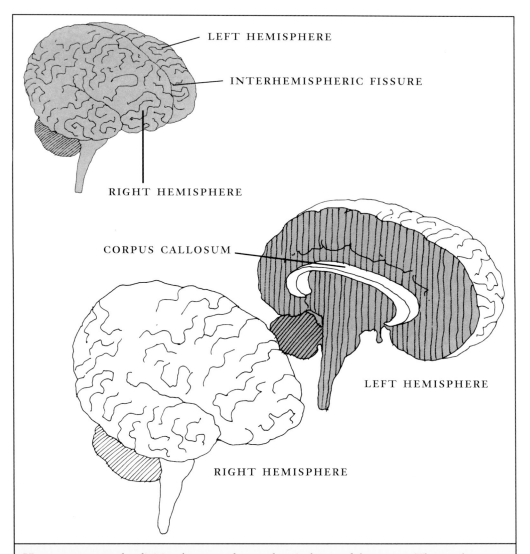

LEFT HEMISPHERE

INTERHEMISPHERIC FISSURE

RIGHT HEMISPHERE

CORPUS CALLOSUM

LEFT HEMISPHERE

RIGHT HEMISPHERE

Here you can see the division between the two hemispheres of the cortex. The crack between them is called the "interhemispheric fissure." The two hemispheres specialize in different mental skills, but brain functions are not as neatly divided as they appear. Phineas's tamping iron struck the left hemisphere first but also grazed the right hemisphere on the way out. He lost something from both hemispheres. *Illustration by David Macaulay*

organ work, the brain's fundamental unit, which is the brain cell, or neuron. You'll need a microscope and a lot of skill to see a single neuron, but all of these structures—the cortex, cerebellum, brain stem, and spinal cord—are made up of neurons specialized to relay and transmit tiny electrical impulses. By layering and connecting billions of neurons, you get a brain.

But by looking at your brain in your hand, you'll notice that the cortex splits in half right down the middle. The left hemisphere and the right hemisphere are separated on top by a deep crack—the interhemispheric fissure—but joined in the middle of the brain by a thick mat of nerves—the corpus callosum. The corpus is the switchboard for signals back and forth between the two halves. In recent times, scientists have learned that the two hemispheres specialize in certain skills. Sometimes you'll hear brain researchers talk about a "right brain" or a "left brain" skill. They really mean right or left hemisphere. But you can't see any skills by looking at the outside of a brain.

Indeed, if you're looking at your brain from the outside, you might wonder if you're holding the cortex backwards. The front of the cortex seems to be hanging in space until you realize that your face fits the space underneath. The part of the cortex above your face is the frontal lobe. The frontal lobe is the part that concerns us most regarding Phineas, but you should know the other lobes—the parietal lobe on top and the occipital lobe at the back of your head, right above your cerebellum. Wrapping around your temples on the side of your head are the temporal lobes. Each hemisphere has its own frontal, parietal, occipital, and temporal lobes. All together, the cortex is a soft mass of folded nerve tissue. It looks as if your cortex was folded up quickly and stuffed in any old way, but the truth is that every human brain is folded in exactly the

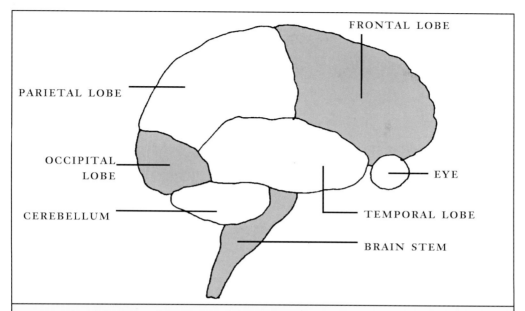

PARIETAL LOBE

FRONTAL LOBE

OCCIPITAL
LOBE

EYE

CEREBELLUM

TEMPORAL LOBE

BRAIN STEM

The brain cortex is like a city; every part has an address. Instead of a city's east or west side, the cortex has a left and right hemisphere. The folds and ridges in the hemispheres are like cross streets, and medical students must memorize every one. The cortex also has four lobes —the frontal (in front), the parietal (on top), the occipital (at the back), and the temporal (on the side). A brain "address" can specify left or right hemisphere, the lobe, the nearest ridge or fold, and whether the location is on top or bottom, inside or out, and front or back. Phineas was injured most seriously on the inside of the left frontal lobe, but scientists are still arguing about the exact address. *Illustration by David Macaulay*

same way. How the neurons inside those folds and ridges connect is what makes every human being singular.

After this tour of the outside of the brain, what you and the Boston doctors in 1850 still lack is a map of the nerve cells. In 1850, the Boston doctors know very little about any kind of cell, even though the cell revolution is getting under way in Germany, thanks to Matthias Schleiden and Theodor Schwann. Working independently, they both revisit the work of Robert Hooke, the microscope observer who came up with the name *cell* in 1665. Hooke, they realize, was seeing empty cork cells because they were dead. Now, for the first time, Schleiden sees living cells in plants. Schwann sees them in animal tissue. Together, they realize that the cell is the fundamental unit of life. Everything alive, from slime molds to human beings, is composed of cells. It is the stuff inside the cell that controls every process of life, from digestion to reproduction.

As a living organism becomes more complex, its cells *differentiate*—that is, they specialize. A line of cells will differentiate and become muscle cells. Another will differentiate and become nerve cells. All complex animals have nerve cells, but no animal has as many nerve cells as humans do. Your brain and spinal cord have about 100 billion neurons.

A neuron is basically a wire with plugs at each end. Unlike most wires, most neurons have many, many plugs so they can both relay messages and switch

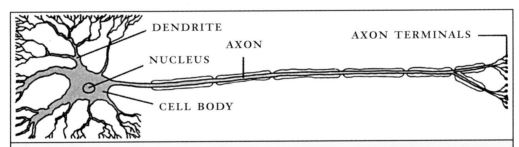

The nerve cell, or neuron, is a living, one-way wire with switches at both ends. Messages arrive chemically in the dendrites, where they are converted to electrical impulses, which travel down the axon, the long body of the cell. At the terminal on the far end, signals are converted back into chemical messengers, called neurotransmitters, for the short voyage across the synapse to the dendrites of the next neuron. Amazingly, neurons can work as fast as thought. *Illustration by David Macaulay*

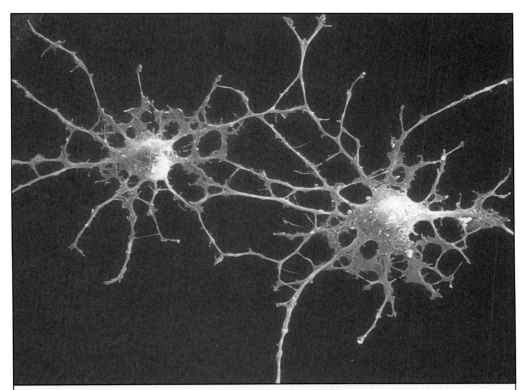

Here two human nerve cells show off their intricate network of axon terminals and dendrites. These connections are so fine that they cannot be seen through a conventional light microscope. A scanning electron microscope (SEM) was used here to capture the details. *SEM photograph by Andrew Leonard, Photo Researchers Inc.*

them. A neuron is a long, skinny cell with a tangle of receivers at one end called dendrites, a long connector called an axon in between, and at the other end a smaller tangle of transmitters called axon terminals. Neurons never actually touch one another or splice together. There is always a tiny gap between the axon terminal of one neuron and the dendrite of the next. The gap is called a synapse. It is bridged by signaling chemicals called neurotransmitters. A message travels as an electrical impulse through the axon, down the body of the nerve cell, to the axon terminal. There the electrical impulse is converted into a chemical neurotransmitter to float across the synapse to the next neuron. Here's where the complications begin. In your brain, your neurons have lots of choices. Your brain has lots of synapses because the neurons are layered and clumped together so that the number of possible connections is huge. Each neuron can have anywhere from 1,000 to 6,000 synapses. That means the 10 billion neurons in your brain and spinal cord have a possible 10 *trillion* synaptic choices to make. Complexity is good. Making synaptic connections is how your brain actually thinks, learns, remembers, acts, and reacts.

The Boston doctors watching Phineas in 1850 haven't a clue about neurons, which won't be discovered for another twenty years. Still, these doctors know that the brain sits atop the spinal cord, a thick, bundled cable of thousands of threads. Doctors do not know that each thread is a bundle of microscopic neurons. They do know that cutting the spinal cord results in paralysis. The higher the break in the spinal cord, the more complete the paralysis. They know that if the cord is cut at the base of the brain stem, the patient dies.

That's why Phineas interests the doctors. His injury is not at the back of his head in the cerebellum or at the bottom of the brain near the brain stem. He was struck through the forehead, and the iron must have pierced the frontal lobe of the cortex. If Phineas survived with a large piece of his cortex destroyed, then what does the cortex do? Across America and Europe, doctors are fiercely divided over this very question. These are the two rival schools. One group thinks the brain is a "whole intelligence," that is, that your brain is one interconnected "mind." Let's call them the "Whole Brainers." They think of the cortex as a chamber holding a formless cloud or jelly driven by a mysterious "vital force." Through this force, every part of the brain is connected to every other part. The Whole Brainers believe that thoughts and commands can originate anywhere in the brain jelly/cloud and flash into action. If one part of the brain is injured, then the functions or thoughts that came from there will flow to another part.

Unfortunately, the Whole Brainers have no hard evidence for their theory. Instead they must look for unusual cases that might back them up. Phineas seems to be such a case. Dr. Bigelow of Harvard thinks so. He is a Whole Brainer.

His opponents believe in "localized function"; that is, they believe that the brain is divided into specific areas that control specific things. Let's call them the "Localizers." They are followers of the Austrian Dr. Gall, who started the brain revolution by declaring that the brain was the seat of intelligence, emotions, and will. Dr. Gall called his brain science "phrenology" (a made-up Greek word). By any name, the Localizers, or Phrenologists, believe that "organs" inside the brain control specific functions. They draw up a model Phrenological Head to show the "organs" in their correct positions. The "Organ of Veneration [respect]" and the "Organ of Benevolence [kindness]," for example, are supposed to be just above the left eyebrow. (Remember where Phineas was hit by the iron? Stay tuned.) Unfortunately, the Phrenologists have no way of knowing which part of the brain controls what. "Benevolence" cannot be seen on the outside of the brain.

Later in the nineteenth century, scientists will discover that a weak electrical current applied to the exposed brain of a laboratory animal will make cer-

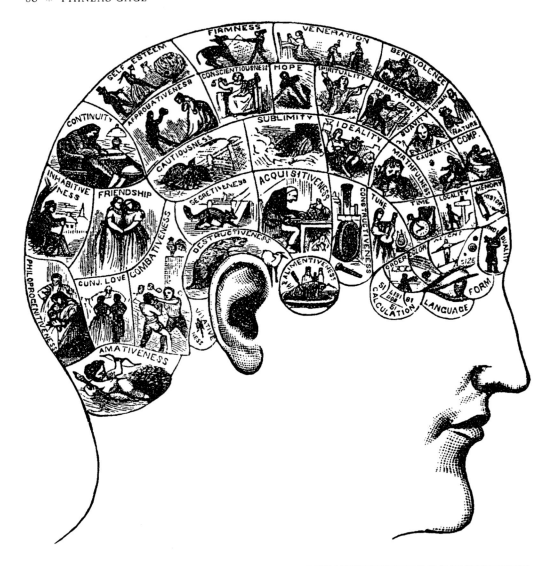

A Phrenological Head is definitely an eye-catcher—bald as a billiard ball and each "organ" carefully outlined and labeled. By the middle of the nineteenth century, a popular parlor game is "reading" one's character by feeling the skull for bumps and dips and then matching them to a head chart such as this one. *Hulton Collection, Getty Images*

tain muscles twitch involuntarily and certain senses sharpen or go dead. In the early twentieth century, scientists will invent more sophisticated and less dangerous ways to "see" brain activity. Eventually they will chart the brain's electrical signals by attaching electrodes to the scalp for an "electroencephalograph," or EEG. The EEG plots amazing patterns of electrical activity that match specific areas of the brain with specific functions. Toward the end of the twentieth century, scientists will invent brain scanners that can "image" the electrical and chemical activity inside a living brain.

Back in 1850, the Localizers/Phrenologists haven't seen a single thought or brainwave. Still, that doesn't stop them from identifying thirty-seven "organs" of the brain. How do they do it? Bumps. That's right. Bumps on the head. The Phrenologists reason that if you have a strong organ, it will be big and project from your skull as a bump. If you have a weak organ, it will be small and you'll have a dip or depression in your skull. Run your hand over your own skull and you will find all sorts of knobs, bumps, dips, and so on. The Phrenologists decide that if you have a bump over your Organ of Amativeness, you are a person with a strong talent for physical love. If you have a dip or a depression over your Organ of Philoprogenitiveness (also known as parental love), you're not going to be fond of children.

Among Boston doctors, phrenology is considered serious stuff when Phineas walks into the middle of the debate of the Whole Brainers versus the Localizers. Both sides seize him as proof of their belief. Dr. Bigelow and his fellow Whole Brainers say that Phineas would surely have died if specific areas of the brain were vital to specific functions. After all, the tamping iron carried away pieces of Phineas's brain. If every part of the brain was vital, then he should be dead. Yet here is Phineas alive in Boston, walking, talking, and taking care of himself. Therefore, say the Whole Brainers, the whole brain must be able to perform any function of one part.

On the other side, Dr. Harlow is a Localizer, or at least he is a friend of some leading Localizers/Phrenologists. The Localizers say Phineas proves their theory. The tamping iron has not killed him because the damage is limited to specific organs that are not critical to life. Yet the Localizers/Phrenologists don't have all the facts. In 1850, when Phineas comes to Boston, Dr. Harlow feels he must keep the details of his patient's personality problems confidential, but he does tell some of the truth to Dr. Nelson Sizer. Dr. Sizer is a big man in phrenology and lectures on it all over New England. Dr. Harlow leaks the information to Dr. Sizer that the "completely recovered" Phineas is not the old Phineas. Dr. Sizer tries to disguise the source of his report to the *American Phrenological Journal* in 1851, writing, "We have been informed by the best authority that after the man recovered, and while recovering, he was grossly profane, coarse, and vulgar, to such a degree that his society was intolerable to decent people."

Dr. Sizer's report is wonderful news for the Localizers/Phrenologists. As Dr. Sizer explains, "If we remember correctly, the iron passed through the regions of the organs of BENEVOLENCE and VENERATION, which left these

An MRI scan allows us to look inside a living person's head and see a slice of everything from the throat to the spinal cord. Inside the brain, you can see the different lobes of the cortex; the corpus callosum, which joins the two hemispheres; the cerebellum at the back of the head; and the brain stem. Compare this to the phrenological chart on page 36.
MRI scan by Scott Canzine and Sue Trainor, Photo Researchers Inc.

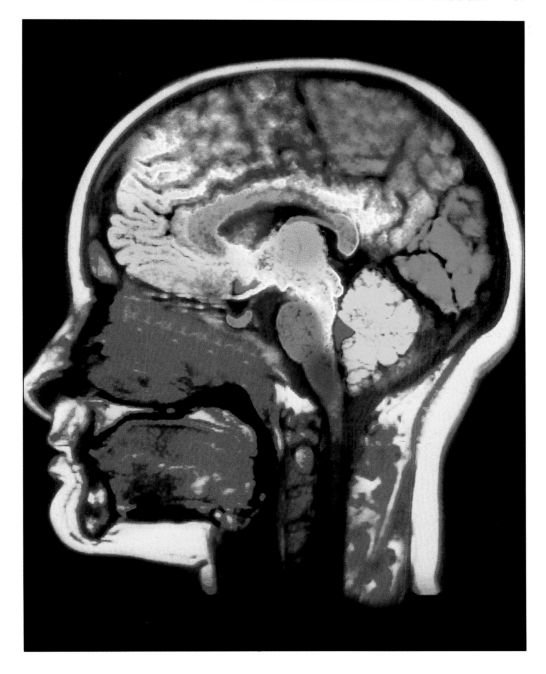

organs without influence in his character, hence his profanity, and want of respect and kindness."

In the long run, the Localizers will turn out to be somewhat right about localization but completely wrong about phrenological organs. The Whole Brainers will turn out to be right about the complex interconnections of the brain but wrong about the brain acting as a whole. The 10 billion neurons in your brain are not connected at random. They are organized into "local circuits" within the cortex; the local circuits form "subcortical nuclei," which together form "cortical regions," which form "systems," which form "systems of systems," which form you.

Specific areas of the brain do control specific functions and behaviors, but it's not always as "logical" as we would imagine. Skills that you think should be in the same brain patch are scattered about in different places in the cortex. Different areas of the cortex let you recognize letters in a book or faces in a crowd, or know whether you are standing upright. Yet many of these localized functions are also controlled by interactions with other parts of the brain. The human brain, it turns out, is both localized and interconnected. We know so much more about the brain today than the Phrenologists and the Whole Brainers did in 1850, yet we really understand only the rough outlines.

Back in 1850, Dr. Bigelow tells the Boston doctors, "Taking all the circum-

---

This ceramic bust by L. N. Fowler was to help serious phrenologists locate the thirty-seven "organs" of the brain while feeling around on the head for bumps and dips. Phrenology lost credibility as science found better ways to probe the brain. Compare this to the "coronal" MRI on page 68. *Photograph by D. Parker, Photo Researchers Inc.*

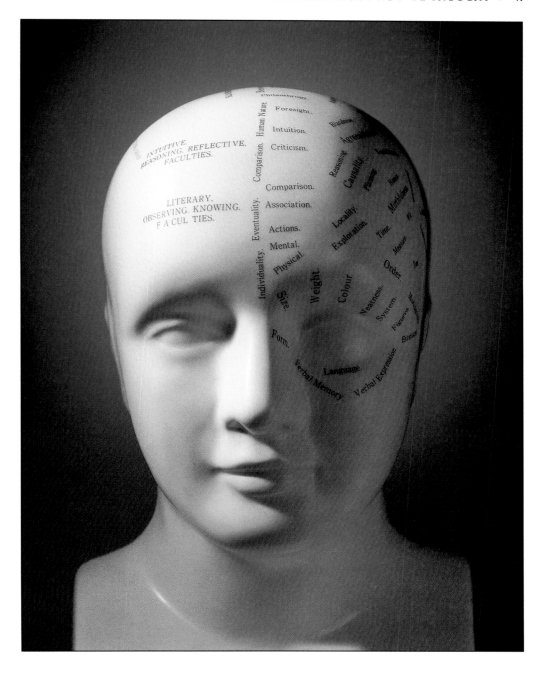

Around 1920, a group of Harvard Medical School students gather around the skull of Phineas Gage. The life-size plaster model of Phineas's head made by Dr. Bigelow stands on the left corner of the table. Time has made the skull fragile, but Phineas Gage's fame still draws visitors to Harvard's Countway Library to look without touching. *Photograph from the Warren Anatomical Museum, Countway Library of Medicine, Harvard Medical School*

stances into consideration, it may be doubted whether the present is not the most remarkable history of injury to the brain which has been recorded." He also announces that Mr. Gage has graciously agreed to donate his famous tamping iron to the Harvard Medical College. Dr. Bigelow donates the plaster head of Phineas to go with it. The plaster head remains in Boston, but Phineas and his tamping iron soon slip out of town.

Following Phineas Gage

The story of Phineas Gage is famous, and when people repeat famous stories they have a tendency to improve them. The famous story about Phineas says that after hanging around the Boston medical school for weeks, he grows bored and restless. Phineas takes back his tamping iron and hits the road, traveling from city to city through New England and ending up at P. T. Barnum's American Museum on Broadway in New York City. Barnum's museum has nothing to do with our modern idea of a museum. It is a freak show.

In Barnum's time, people will pay to see "living giants," "bearded ladies," and calves born with two heads. People have always gawked at strange and unusual things. Barnum's special genius is "improving" the unusual. Hype and humbug make Barnum's museum a roaring success. He pulls in the crowds with half-fakes like the "Woolly Horse," a strange, long-haired horse that Barnum declares is a newly discovered species, being part deer, buffalo, elephant, camel, and sheep. At least the Woolly Horse is a real horse. Barnum's "mermaid" is a total fake, a counterfeit fossil pasted together from bones, withered skins, and who knows what else. Barnum shows his "mermaid" alongside real exotic animals like orangutans and grizzly bears. Barnum floods the exterior with the brightest lights in all of New York. Inside, the lighting is deliberately dim. The noise is deafening, with actors, jugglers, and glass blowers working the crowd.

In this wild scene, would anyone notice an ordinary-looking young man with a bad scar on his forehead holding an iron rod? It is said that Phineas exhibited himself and his tamping iron at Barnum's. The most colorful description of Phineas at Barnum's museum comes from Alton Blackington, a Boston radio and TV reporter who broadcasts his account a century after Phineas's death. Blackington says that Barnum's museum billed Phineas as "The Only Living Man With a Hole in His Head." According to Blackington, "The poster and one-sheets depicted a husky young man smiling broadly in spite of a huge iron bar which stuck out of his head. Actually, of course, the iron bar no longer protruded from Gage's head but he had it with him, and another skull, also perforated. During his sideshow performances, he would shove the long iron through the holes in his extra skull to demonstrate just how he was

Phineas Gage's mother said her son exhibited himself here at P. T. Barnum's American Museum on Broadway in New York City. Barnum was the gaudiest showman and greatest hoaxer of his age. Did Phineas Gage, The Man with a Hole in His Head, fit in with the other human oddities and strange wonders that Barnum promoted here with hype and hoopla? *Photograph circa 1850 from the Hulton Collection, Getty Images*

injured. All the details were to be found in a pamphlet he sold, and by paying ten cents extra, skeptics could part Gage's hair and see his brain, what there was left of it, pulsating beneath the new, thin covering."

Blackington spins a great yarn. Unfortunately, we don't know if the details are true. Phineas's mother did tell Dr. Harlow that after leaving Boston, Phineas and his tamping iron visited "most of the larger New England towns and New York, remaining a while in the latter place at Barnum's with his iron." But that's as far as the details go, and Blackington's sources can't be found. In our time, Professor Malcolm Macmillan, an Australian psychologist who is the world's leading expert on Phineas Gage, makes a massive effort to track down the story. Professor Macmillan turns to experts on Barnum, old newspaper files, contemporary diaries, and circus museums. He can't find Phineas anywhere. As far as Professor Macmillan can determine, Dr. Harlow is the only reliable source. Dr. Harlow says that after Phineas leaves Boston in 1850 he gets information about his former patient only from Phineas's mother.

Her name is Hannah Trusell Swetland Gage. She says that Phineas returns from New York to the family's New Hampshire home early in 1851 to work for Mr. Jonathan Currier in his livery stable in the nearby town of Hanover. Whatever Phineas's problems with people, he gets on well with horses. He works in Currier's stable for a year and a half. His health is good, his mother remembers. He seems happiest with children and animals. Then, in 1852, he meets a stranger in Hanover who has big plans to set up a stagecoach line in South America between Valparaiso and Santiago, Chile. He could use a man who is experienced with horses. In August 1852, Phineas leaves New England forever, bound for Chile and a new life as a stagecoach driver.

Here the evidence fades out for a time. His mother recalls only that Phineas talked about driving six-horse teams for this coach line on the bottom of the world. She doesn't recall the stranger's name. But there is a small clue in the August 1852 order books of the Abbott-Downing Company of Concord, New

Hampshire. In 1852, Abbott-Downing makes the finest and toughest stage-coach in the world. This Concord coach is the famous Wild West stage, hauling mail and passengers over the plains and across deserts. In 1852, the Abbott-Downing Company books show that a Mr. James McGill ordered a Concord stage for a new coach line that he was organizing in Valparaiso, Chile. Was James McGill the stranger who hired Phineas? Professor Macmillan is still looking for evidence in New Hampshire or Chile, but he says it's possible.

A Concord stagecoach is a monster on huge wooden wheels. With six horses, nine passengers, an armed guard, mail, and freight, a fully loaded Concord stage is over six tons in motion. The driver controls it all with reins, a whip, and a feeble wooden foot brake. It's not an easy job. The driver's fists are filled with reins, three pair in the left hand for the "near" side horses, three in the right for the "off" side. The whip is largely for making showy, whip-cracking arrivals in town. Mostly he drives with his hands and voice, using the matched pairs of horses to wheel, to slow down, or to pull clear.

Until Professor Macmillan turns up solid proof, we can't say for sure if Phineas drives a Concord stagecoach in Chile, but the driver's job would be much the same on any six-horse coach—hard, tiring, and sometimes exciting. According to his mother, Phineas drives for nearly seven years on a regular schedule over the primitive roads between Valparaiso and Santiago. There is so much we would like to know but probably never will about Phineas's time in Chile. Does he—can he—learn Spanish? Is he a loner? Does he stay with the same stage line or jump from job to job? Does he tell anyone in Chile his tragic story?

If we can't know any of this, we can catch a glimpse of Phineas in the driver's

Although it is being pulled by four horses instead of the usual six, this is a New Hampshire–built Concord stagecoach, somewhere in Chile at about the time that Phineas Gage arrived there. We have no way of knowing if it is Phineas at the reins. *New Hampshire Historical Society*

seat, his fists full of reins, his face full of dust, his hat pulled down over his eyes against the Chilean sun. Phineas is intent on his team, on the slope of the road, and on the big, rocking coach. His decisions are quick and instinctive, based on long habit. He knows his horses. He knows his reins.

We know one other thing about Phineas in Chile. He has his tamping iron with him. Stowed under the seat or ready to hand, the tamping iron goes everywhere Phineas goes.

In 1859, Phineas washes up on his family's doorstep in San Francisco. His mother has moved to California from New Hampshire to be with her youngest daughter, Phebe, and her new husband, David Shattuck. In July, a very sick Phineas gets off a boat in San Francisco and somehow finds his way to the Shattuck house. Phineas is in "feeble condition," his mother says, much changed since she last saw him in New Hampshire. Phineas tells his mother that he is only suffering from the voyage. He had been terribly seasick on his first voyage from Boston to Chile in 1852, he tells her. He will get over this. It takes months, but he seems to fully recover.

In San Francisco, Phineas is not a good invalid. He hates resting. He has worked hard all his life, on the family farm, on the railroad, in the livery stable, and on the Chilean stagecoaches. As Phineas gradually feels better, he wants to go right out and get back to work. Finally Phineas takes a job plowing for a farmer near the little town of Santa Clara. Phineas tell his mother that he has no trouble with the farm work, but he soon quarrels with the farmer. He moves to another farm, then another. Phineas is "always finding something which did not suit him in every place he tried," says his mother. That February, he is back in San Francisco for a visit. At the dinner table, he suddenly falls into "a fit."

A fit is an epileptic seizure. Epilepsy is not a disease but a complex of symptoms. Basically, a seizure is an electrical storm in your brain's nerve cells. It can begin in one area of the brain and spread to other regions, sometimes sending your muscles into involuntary convulsions. Seizures are relatively common; about one person in 200 will experience a seizure, mild or severe, at some time in life. But an epileptic seizure is only a symptom; the cause can be anything from a tumor, to an inherited genetic disposition to seizures, to a blow to the head. In our time, we control most epileptic symptoms with powerful drugs called "anticonvulsants," because uncontrolled seizures can cause their own brain damage.

In 1860, severe epileptic seizures are not controllable. All the doctors in San

By the time a seasick Phineas Gage staggered ashore here in 1859, San Francisco was still a frontier town on the farthest edge of the continent. *Photograph from the San Francisco History Center, San Francisco Public Library*

Francisco can offer Phineas are theories, useless drugs, and nursing instructions. After that first seizure at his sister's dinner table, he recovers almost immediately with no memory of the fit or any ill effect. Within hours, he has two more seizures. In the morning, he wakes up feeling like his old self and insists that he has to get back to work. Back in Santa Clara, he switches farm jobs again. In May, he comes into San Francisco to visit his mother. He seems fine. Two days later, at five o'clock in the morning, Phineas has a severe seizure. Then he has another and another. The intervals between seizures grow shorter and shorter.

The family physician comes and "bleeds" him. By 1860, the practice of bleeding a patient is the last gasp of a treatment that goes back to the "bodily humors" theory of the ancient Greeks. The doctor who treats Phineas decides he has too much blood and draws off the "extra." It's outmoded treatment, even for 1860. Back in Vermont in 1848, Dr. Harlow bled Phineas at the height of his fever. Without understanding why, Dr. Harlow may have helped Phineas at that moment of crisis. Drawing blood reduces blood pressure slightly, which may have taken some of the pressure off his swollen brain. But bleeding does nothing for epileptic seizures.

Phineas's seizures are probably caused by slow changes in brain tissue damaged in the original accident. Why the damage worsens as Phineas grows older is unknown. Possibly Phineas strikes his head again. Perhaps the constant jarring in the driver's seat of a lumbering stagecoach causes a concussion on the site of the old damage. Perhaps Phineas has a low-grade bacterial infection or perhaps a brain tumor. No one can say why, but now Phineas's seizures grow more violent and more frequent. One after another, the seizures leave him weaker and weaker.

They finally kill him on May 21, 1860, at his sister's house in San Francisco. The immediate cause of death is probably hypothermia—his body can't control its internal temperature. In our time, we read about hypothermia killing mountain climbers, or sailors who fall into cold water. An epileptic seizure creates the same effect as shivering in icy water. In cold water, you shiver—your muscles spasm—to heat up your body. While shivering violently in cold water, you don't realize you are also sweating as your muscles throw off heat. Eventually the muscles expel heat faster than it can be replaced. Your blood temperature starts to fall. Your internal organs, especially the brain and heart, need a constant core temperature to function. As the brain detects a fall in blood temperature, it automatically protects itself by shutting down the blood supply to the hands and feet. You lose feeling. If you keep losing heat, the brain shuts down blood circulation over a larger and larger area of your skin. Phineas's muscle seizures are causing the same effect. His brain shuts down circulation to his feet and hands, then his skin, and then organ by organ until his brain must choose between blood for itself and blood for the heart. His heart stops. This is how Phineas dies, twenty days short of his thirty-seventh birthday.

He is buried at Laurel Hill Cemetery in San Francisco. Phineas is a stranger in the city, and few outside his family circle know anything about his curious past. No California newspaper notes his death or burial. Family news travels slowly across the continent. Back east, the country is drifting toward Civil War, and when it breaks out the following April, doctors soon have more pressing concerns than Phineas Gage.

Half the world away from San Francisco in 1862, French surgeon Paul Broca in Paris announces a discovery that finally turns brain theory into brain science. Dr. Broca shows how damage to one very small spot in the brain causes one very specific kind of damage. Broca is still unable to study a living brain, but he has been performing autopsies on the brains of stroke victims. A

stroke is an interruption of the blood supply to the brain that causes localized damage and often leaves stroke patients without the ability to speak. Broca notices that in the brains of stroke patients who'd lost the power to speak there is visible damage in a small area on the outside of the left frontal lobe.

The spot becomes famous as "Broca's area." To find it, put your hand on the top of your left ear, directly above your ear hole. Move your fingers about two inches forward. Underneath the skull is your "Broca's area." If it's damaged, you will lose the ability to speak. In medical language, you will have "aphasia." Soon after Broca's announcement, a German named Carl Wernicke identifies a second area on the left temporal lobe that separately controls the ability to understand speech. The loss of the ability to understand what is said to you is called "receptive aphasia." Who could have imagined that these two skills would be controlled from two different places in the brain? Broca's and Wernicke's areas are the first anatomical proof of localization. Other brain researchers soon learn to use low-voltage electricity to stimulate specific points on the brain. Bit by bit, the map of the brain grows more detailed and more localized.

The new scientific map of the brain has no relation to our old friend the Phrenological Head. Phrenology falls into disgrace, even though the Phrenol-

The unquiet grave of Phineas Gage was disturbed once in 1867 by Dr. Harlow and then again in 1940 by the rapidly growing city. San Francisco needed the land under the old pioneer cemetery where he was buried. The remains of Phineas, his mother, his brother-in-law, and 35,000 other San Francisco pioneers were dug up by the city and moved to a mass grave in a suburban cemetery. Their headstones and tombs were trucked away for landfill. In 1944, a strong coastal storm uncovered the missing tombstones under a highway, and these boys scrambled up to see. If Phineas Gage had a tombstone, it was somewhere in this stone pile. *Photograph from the San Francisco History Center, San Francisco Public Library*

ogists were right about localization. The Whole Brainers are also shaken. If speech is localized on these two spots, how could someone with massive frontal lobe injuries—Phineas Gage, for example—speak? And yet Dr. Harlow had said that Phineas had fully recovered. Of course, few doctors in Boston remember much about the Gage case, and even Dr. Harlow has lost track of Phineas.

By the time Dr. Harlow finds Phineas again, he is too late. After Phineas leaves for South America in 1852, Dr. Harlow's contact with the Gage family is broken. Quietly, he has wondered what became of his most celebrated patient. Then in 1866, the year after the Civil War ends, Dr. Harlow, now running a small practice in Woburn, Massachusetts, finds an address for Hannah Gage in San Francisco. He writes to her, and his letter makes the long trek across America. Mrs. Gage is delighted to hear from the doctor who'd done so much for her son. Unfortunately, she has the sad duty to report his death six years before.

It is too late for an autopsy, and California is too far for a research visit. But Dr. Harlow doesn't give up. They exchange cordial letters. Mrs. Gage describes Phineas's last illness. She fills in the details of his life after he left the medical spotlight in Boston. She recalls how Phineas was extremely fond of his little nephews and nieces. Dr. Harlow notes her description of how Phineas would entertain them "with the most fabulous recitals of his wonderful feats and hair-breadth escapes, without any foundation except in his fancy." Dr. Harlow concludes that Phineas had "a great fondness for children, horses, and dogs—only exceeded by his attachment for his tamping iron, which was his constant companion during the remainder of his life."

Finally, Dr. Harlow makes an unusual request. Explaining the importance

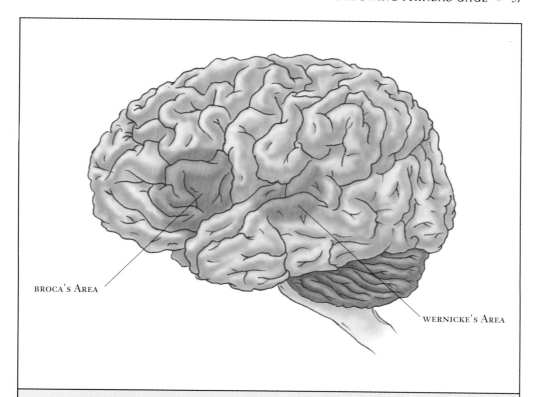

BROCA'S AREA

WERNICKE'S AREA

In 1862, Paul Broca found an area on the lower left frontal lobe that controlled the ability to speak. The discovery of Broca's area finished off the theories of the Phrenologists and the Whole Brainers. Soon after, Carl Wernicke found another area on the left temporal lobe that controlled the ability to understand speech. *Illustration by Jerry Malone*

of her son's case to science, Dr. Harlow recalls how many scoffed at Phineas when Dr. Bigelow first presented his case in Boston. Now there is a way to settle the question, Dr. Harlow explains. Would Mrs. Gage allow her son's body to be exhumed—dug up—from his grave? Would she allow the skull to be removed and shipped to Massachusetts?

What a request. Surely Dr. Harlow must be held in the highest regard by

In his later years, Dr. John Martyn Harlow became an important man in Woburn, a state senator, an advisor to the governor, and a bank president. When he died in 1907, he left his large estate to various charities, including Middlesex County Medical Society. In 1998, the society had enough of Dr. Harlow's money left to help pay for the bronze monument to Phineas Gage on the town green in Cavendish, Vermont. *Countway Library of Medicine, Harvard Medical School*

Hannah Gage. Why else would she consent? With her son-in-law and the mayor of San Francisco, who happens to be a physician, standing by as witnesses, Phineas's coffin is uncovered and carried to a shed. There, Dr. J. D. B. Stillman, a local surgeon, removes the skull. The huge fracture on the forehead is unmistakable. Dr. Stillman removes something else from the coffin— the tamping iron that Phineas carried everywhere, even to his grave. That December, David Shattuck takes the skull and tamping iron with him when he travels east on business. Early in the new year, he hands them over to an extremely grateful and very excited Dr. Harlow in Massachusetts.

At last Dr. Harlow is at liberty to tell the full story of Phineas Gage's "recovery" twenty years before. He appears before the Massachusetts Medical Society in 1868 and spills the beans. "This case has been cited as one of complete recovery . . . without any impairment to the intellect," he says, but in truth, Phineas's personality changed drastically after the accident. "Previous to his injury, though untrained in the schools, he possessed a well-balanced mind, and was looked upon by those who knew him as a shrewd, smart business man, very energetic and persistent in executing all his plans of operation. In this regard, his mind was radically changed, so decidedly that his friends and acquaintances said he was 'no longer Gage.'"

Phineas went from being "the most efficient and capable foreman" on the railroad to a man who couldn't be trusted because he couldn't get along with anyone. The new Phineas was pigheaded and stubborn one moment and wishy-washy and vague the next. "I think you have been shown that the subsequent history and progress of the case only warrant us in saying that physically, the recovery was quite complete," says Dr. Harlow. "Mentally the recovery certainly was only partial." The new Phineas could walk, drive a team of horses, and sail away to Chile, but he had lost a vital skill—he no longer knew how to be social.

Being social is a hard skill to measure. Social behavior goes beyond the ability to activate the correct muscles or decode the right spoken sounds. It's different from having manners. Manners are learned, and they differ greatly from culture to culture. Your parents teach you the "right" way to eat or to greet strangers, but other parents in other countries teach their children other "right" ways. Forks or chopsticks or fingers, there's no "right" way to put food in your mouth, yet all humans swallow the same way. Swallowing is automatic behavior. Using a fork is learned behavior. Eating politely in the company of others is social behavior.

In your brain, Broca's area may let you speak and Wernicke's area may let you understand, but listening is also a complicated social behavior. Whether you realize it or not, you've been taught how to listen—how to make or break eye contact, how to murmur agreement or quiet objection, how to smile at the right moment or not to smile at all if the subject is grave. You also know how to show (or hide) your emotional reactions. You can laugh or yawn, roll your eyes upward in boredom, or open your eyes wide in delight. All of these behaviors can mean something entirely different in another culture, but all cultures have listening behavior.

It's hard to believe that this tamping iron shot through the skull without killing Phineas Gage. Dr. Harlow had their picture taken together in 1868 to document his case. *Glennon Collection, Woburn Public Library, by permission of the Trustees of the Library*

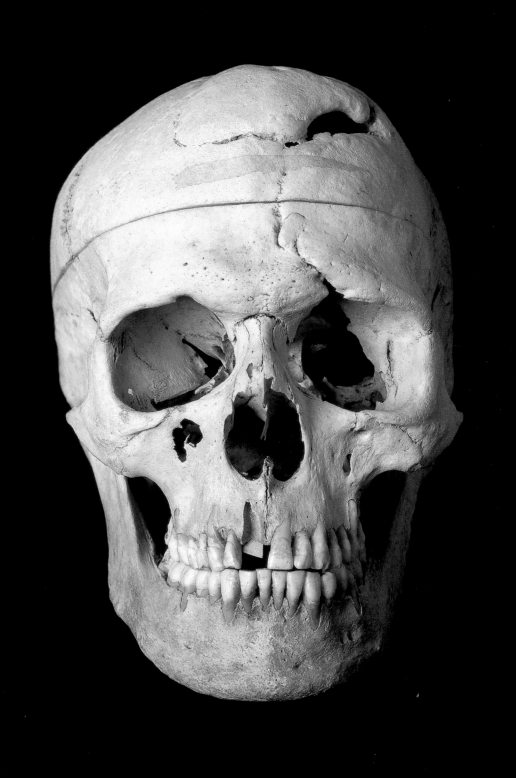

To act human, you mix emotions, actions, routines, customs, manners, words, and expressions in a predictable way. That's what Phineas seems to have lost. Bossing a railroad construction gang requires more than a loud voice. A gang has to be able to "read" the social behavior of the foreman. They have to know if he's angry or just joking, if his orders are reasonable, or if his judgment can be trusted. He has to be able to "read" the social behavior of his men, to know who are the reliable ones and who are the troublemakers. By all reports, the old Phineas was an excellent foreman. The new Phineas was not. All these changes were brought on by a hole through a specific part of his brain.

In Boston twenty years before, the central exhibit had been Phineas himself, alive and seemingly well. Now Dr. Harlow reveals the clincher—his skull. He has "prepared" it for inspection, carefully sawing through the bone at just above eyebrow level so the top of the cranium can be lifted off. Now his audience can see the hole in the top of his mouth through which the rod passed. The top of Phineas's skull is an amazing sight. The doctors can see where Dr. Harlow pushed two large fragments back into place and how the edges started to regrow, unmistakable proof that Phineas survived the trauma and that his body started to heal the damage. Yet there is a visible hole in the top, a small triangular opening the size of a quarter, where the iron either smashed or carried away the bone completely. The skin closed over it, but for eleven years, Phineas had a real hole in his head.

In death, Phineas's skull revealed the unmistakable signs of his terrible accident. Today, Phineas's skull, tamping iron, and life mask are exhibited at Harvard Medical School.
Photograph by Doug Mindell, skull courtesy of the Countway Library of Medicine, Harvard Medical School

At last, the true story of Phineas Gage is out in the open. The scientific debate about the brain, though, has moved on. The theories of the Localizers and Whole Brainers are being replaced by a new experimental brain science. In time, the pinpointing of control areas will become more and more detailed. Knowledge of cells in general and neurons in particular will transform understanding of the brain. Yet the truth about Phineas poses a question that no one seems eager to answer. If there are exact locations in the brain that allow for the ability to hear or to breathe, is there a place that generates human social behavior? If that place is damaged, do you stop acting human?

Putting Phineas Together Again

In our time, Phineas Gage is a textbook case. Students of neurology or psychology study his case because it illustrates how the lobes of the frontal cortex—the two halves of your brain that meet in your forehead—are the seat of "executive functions." Those are your abilities to predict, to decide, and to interact socially.

Unfortunately, Phineas is not the only person to have suffered damage to the frontal cortex. Antonio and Hanna Damasio, a husband-and-wife team of doctors, regularly see people who remind them of Phineas Gage. The Damasios are renowned brain researchers at the University of Iowa Hospitals & Clinics in Iowa City and treat patients with the same kind of frontal lobe damage that afflicted Phineas. Like Phineas, these patients with frontal lobe damage have trouble making decisions. Like Phineas with his $1,000 pebbles, they perform well on logic and math tests but make strange choices in trading situations. Their emotional responses are unpredictable. They seem out of step emotionally with the rest of the world.

The patients who come to the Damasios' clinic are not victims of blasting accidents. Their brain injuries usually follow surgery to remove a tumor from deep inside the frontal cortex. This kind of brain surgery is strictly a last resort to save a patient's life, because even if the operation goes well, the risk of side effects is high. Any damage to the frontal cortex can change behavior and personality forever, as the case of Phineas Gage demonstrates. Sometimes, cancer surgeons have no other choice. These cases are not common, but the Damasios have seen a dozen patients with many of the same symptoms as Phineas. All have frontal cortex damage. All have trouble making decisions on personal or social matters. All react with little empathy and seem to find emotion a foreign language.

To study these modern-day Phineases, the Damasios have far more sophisticated equipment than Dr. Harlow did. They have the full arsenal of CTs and MRIs—noninvasive brain scanners that can electronically "slice up" a brain and lay it out, level by level, like the floor plan of a house. But the Damasios also do simpler tests. Emotional response is difficult to measure, but there is one usually reliable sign of how you are feeling—sweaty palms. When your emotions are "aroused," your skin (all over and not just your palms) gets slightly warmer and slightly sweatier. Your sweat contains salts, which increase electrical conductivity. A person having a strong emotional reaction is going to "spike" a conductivity meter. It's the same principle used in the police "lie detector" test, only the Damasios are interested in a different sort of truth.

Hooked to a skin response machine, the modern-day Phineases are shown a series of emotionally charged pictures—a tranquil landscape, a beautiful woman, a severed foot. Their skin reactions are usually the same—nearly flat. The emotional colors of their world seem to have drained away. Another Damasio experiment involves a computer "gambling" game. There are four decks: A, B, C, and D. The decks are rigged. Normal subjects who play the game soon figure out that the C and D decks are better risks than A and B. The modern-day Phineases keep playing A and B, though they can explain to the experimenters mathematically exactly why C and D are better risks. They realize the game is rigged to favor a "slow but steady" strategy against a "risk-all" strategy, but they still play "risk-all." Call them Phineas's rules.

So what part of the brain controls this behavior? Dr. Harlow thought he had found the precise location of Phineas's troubles once he had the skull. By then, Phineas's actual brain was long gone, but Dr. Harlow knew enough gross anatomy to calculate that the iron had passed through the very front of the left frontal cortex. His answer was good enough for 1868. It isn't good enough today.

Studying the brain scans of these Phineas-like patients, the Damasios wonder what a brain scan of Phineas Gage himself would have shown. In 1994, Hanna Damasio has an idea of how to construct one retroactively. First she asks Dr. Albert Galaburda at the Harvard Medical School to have another look at Phineas's skull in the Harvard medical museum. Under the careful eye of

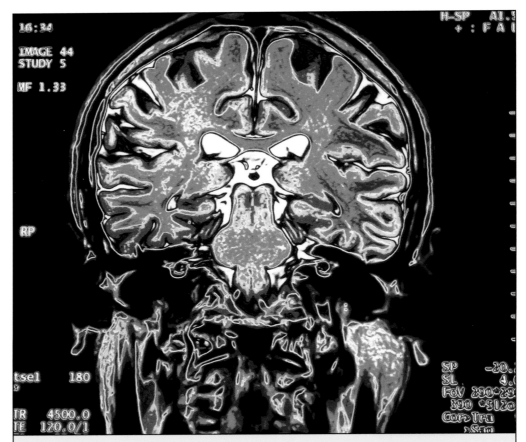

This is a "coronal" MRI. Instead of a side view, this is a slice of the brain taken head-on. Here we're somewhere in the middle of the head with the cortex above, the corpus callosum in the middle, and the brain stem descending to the spinal column. *MRI brain scan by G. Tompkinson, Photo Researchers Inc.*

the curators, Dr. Galaburda x-rays, photographs, and remeasures the skull. The results are digitized so the specifics of Phineas's skull can be overlaid onto a three-dimensional computer image of a generic human skull. Back in her lab in Iowa, Hanna Damasio carefully plots the entrance and exit wounds. A line

is drawn between their center point to lay out a hypothetical path for the tamping iron. The generic electronic skull is then adjusted to Phineas's specifica-
tions. Now Dr. Damasio has Phineas's skull on a computer screen. She can tilt
and rotate it in any direction exactly as if she were holding it in her hand.

Then she adds the tamping iron electronically. The real one tapers, but the
electronic one is represented as a cylinder as big around as the fat end of the
tamping iron. Now Dr. Damasio turns to a computer program called Brainvox
that is used to reassemble brain scan "slices" into a three-dimensional model.
Brainvox fits this electronically scanned brain inside Phineas's electronic skull.

The brain is a very small place, and a very small change in the path of the
iron would have had very different results. Brainvox calculates sixteen possible
paths for the iron to follow through Phineas's head. The anatomical evidence
from Phineas rules out nine of these. Dr. Damasio knows that the iron missed
his jawbone, lightly clipped the interior arch of his brow, and knocked out one
molar but didn't destroy the socket. Any path that falls outside those landmarks
is out of bounds. Of the remaining seven routes, two would have cut important blood vessels and would have killed Phineas instantly. Brainvox lays out
the last five routes. The Damasio team whittles it down to one.

Brainvox plots it as a red cylinder passing through the animated computer
skull. The top of the skull is open to show the rod emerging from the frontal
cortex. It is a riveting image. The scientific journal *Science* puts Brainvox's
images of the pierced skull on its cover and it causes a sensation. Whether
you're a brain surgeon or a sixth-grader, the first time you see the Brainvox
image of Phineas's head with that red bar through it, you wince.

If you study the animated skull from different angles, you can see Phineas's incredible luck. The iron passes through his head at a very steep angle. That's both his salvation and his ruin. It misses a number of key areas on the side and top of the brain. On the left temple, it misses Broca's area for speech. On top, it misses two key sections of the cortex, the motor and somatosensory strips. These areas integrate your sensory input and muscle actions so you keep oriented in space and in motion. Thus Phineas is left with the ability to keep his balance, to focus his attention, and to remember both old and new events.

The tamping iron, however, plows on through his frontal lobes, passing through the middle, where the two hemispheres face each other. The iron damages the left hemisphere more than the right, the front of the frontal cortex more than the back, the underside more than the top. Dr. Damasio recognizes the pattern. Phineas's reconstructed brain matches brain scans of her patients who had cortex tumor surgery.

Humans have always argued about what makes us human. Is it our ability to walk on two feet? To hold tools in our hands? To speak and hear language? To worship a supreme being? The case of Phineas Gage suggests that we are human because our frontal lobes are set up so we can get along with other humans. We are "hard wired" to be sociable. When we lose that ability, we end up like Phineas. His closest companion was an iron rod.

The tamping iron and skull of Phineas have a new home at Harvard Medical

The skull of Phineas Gage appeared on the cover of the journal *Science*. Generated by computer, the red bar plots the exact path of the tamping iron through his frontal cortex. *From Damasio, H., Grabowski, T., Galaburda, A. M., "The return of Phineas Gage: Clues from the brain of a famous patient," Science, 264:1102–1156, 1994. Department of Image Analysis Facility, University of Iowa. Reprinted with permission of the American Association for the Advancement of Science, copyright 1994*

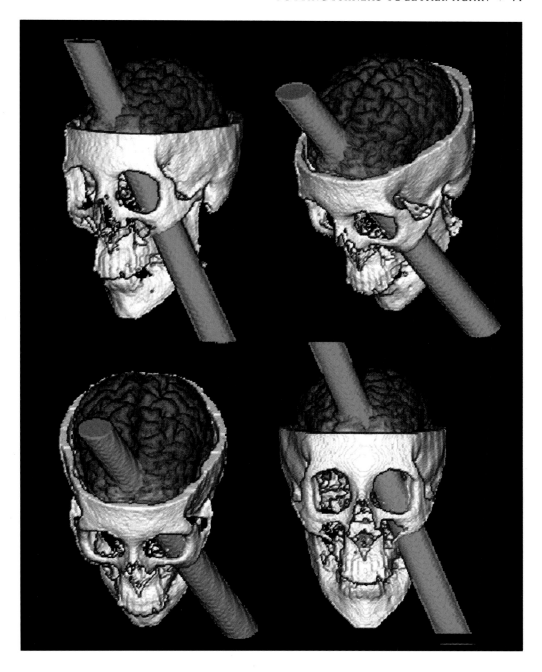

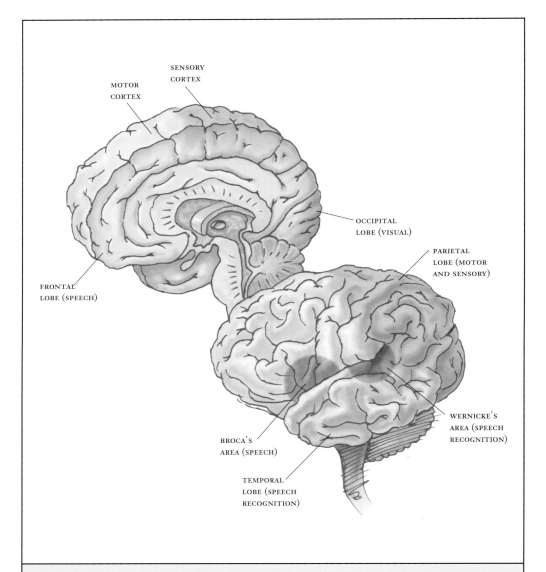

MOTOR
CORTEX

SENSORY
CORTEX

OCCIPITAL
LOBE (VISUAL)

PARIETAL
LOBE (MOTOR
AND SENSORY)

FRONTAL
LOBE (SPEECH)

WERNICKE'S
AREA (SPEECH
RECOGNITION)

BROCA'S
AREA (SPEECH)

TEMPORAL
LOBE (SPEECH
RECOGNITION)

What is so remarkable about Phineas Gage's injury is not only where the rod went in his head but where it did *not* go. The tamping iron missed a number of key areas on either side of the brain that control important functions, including Broca's and Wernicke's areas, plus the motor strip and the somatosensory strip. *Illustration by Jerry Malone*

Look closely to read the inscription on the famous iron: "This is the bar that was shot through the head of Mr. Phineas Gage at Cavendish, Vermont, Sept. 14, 1848. He fully recovered from the injury and deposited this bar in the museum of the Medical College of Harvard University." Someone— either Dr. Harlow or the engraver—got the date wrong. The accident was on September 13, not 14. *Photograph by Doug Mindell; tamping iron courtesy of the Countway Library of Medicine, Harvard Medical School*

School in Boston.

After 150 years on display just outside the dean's office in the medical school, they were cleaned up and moved in 2000 to a new exhibit case in the Countway Library of Medicine just down Shattuck Street. If you want to see Phineas, you have to ask permission at the library's front desk, but generally they will send you straight up to the fifth floor, where Phineas resides in Harvard's collection of medical curiosities.

The Harvard curators say that other museums, such as the Smithsonian Institution, are constantly asking to borrow Phineas's skull and iron, but his traveling days are over. The last time he was lent for exhibit in 1998, he came back with a loosened tooth. That year, Phineas went in the back seat of a limousine to Cavendish, Vermont, for a festival and medical seminar to mark the 150th anniversary of his terrible accident. Psychologists, surgeons, and neurologists came from all over the world to present scientific papers on frontal cortex injuries. Also on hand were men and women in wheelchairs who suffer from cortex injury or disease. To these special attendees, Phineas was no specimen or historical curiosity. He was a fellow sufferer.

At the end of the celebration, the town unveiled a boulder of Vermont granite on the village green with a bronze plaque as a permanent memorial to Phineas. If you go to Vermont, you can read it yourself. It explains what happened in Cavendish, what happened to Phineas, and what happened to Dr. Harlow. It explains what happened to our knowledge of the brain as a result.

The plaque does not answer the question of Phineas's luck. I said at the

In 1998, one hundred and fifty years after his terrible accident, the town of Cavendish, Vermont, held a medical seminar and festival to honor Phineas Gage. The climax was the dedication of a memorial plaque explaining what had happened to Phineas and to brain science as a result. *Photograph by Amy Flynn*

This Concord stagecoach ended its days in Bulawayo, Zimbabwe, Africa, far from the New Hampshire factory where it was made. Phineas Gage ended his days in San Francisco, far from New Hampshire, where he was born; far from Vermont, where he was injured; and far from Chile, where he drove a Concord stagecoach like this one. *New Hampshire Historical Society*

beginning that you could decide for yourself what kind of luck he had at the end. This is what I think: Phineas Gage was lucky. His accident was terrible. It changed him into someone else, and yet Phineas figured out how to live as that new person for eleven years. He was limited in ways that are important to all human beings, but he found a way to live, working with horses. He took care of himself. He saw the world. He died with his family around him, the only people who knew both the old and new Phineas. And he drove a six-horse stagecoach. I bet Phineas Gage drove fast.

Glossary

abscess—a swollen pocket in tissue where dead bacteria and immune cells collect during an infection.

aphasia—the inability to speak, usually caused by injury or disease affecting Broca's area on the brain's frontal lobe.

bacteria—one-celled microorganisms that thrive in virtually every environment on earth, as well as within larger organisms. Bacteria perform a wide variety of actions beneficial to humans, from decomposing organic matter to leavening bread. Only a small percentage of species are *pathogenic*, that is, capable of causing disease in humans.

brain stem—the bottom part of the brain that links to the spinal cord and controls such involuntary functions as breathing, heart rate, and reflex reactions.

cadaver—a dead body donated for dissection.

carbolic acid—a strong, corrosive chemical poison once used as a disinfectant.

cerebellum—the part of the brain located at the back of the head beneath the occipital lobe that regulates involuntary muscles controlling balance and muscle tension.

corpus callosum—a bundle of neurons that connects the left and right hemispheres of the cortex.

daguerreotype—an early photographic process that created a positive image on a metal plate, replaced in the 1860s by glass plate and colloid films that produced negatives.

derrick—a crane for lifting heavy objects.

electroencephalograph (EEG)—an instrument that traces electrical patterns in the brain.

epilepsy—a seizure disorder caused by breakdowns in the natural electrical patterns of the brain.

ether—Ethers are a class of organic compounds, but the "ether" used in the first anesthesia operations was an ether of sulfuric acid and ethyl alcohol. The fumes quickly put surgical patients to sleep, but this ether also had a tendency to stop their breathing completely. It was quickly replaced by less dangerous chemicals.

fermentation—the breakdown by living yeast bacteria of natural sugars into alcohol and carbon dioxide.

frontal lobe—the part of the cortex at the front of the brain.

gangrene—a life-threatening infection occurring when dead and dying tissue close off the circulation of blood to limbs.

hypothermia—a physiological state in which body temperature falls well below normal.

interhemispheric fissure—the space that divides the left and right hemispheres of the cortex.

microorganisms—extremely small living things composed of one or a few cells that can be seen only through a microscope.

neuron—a nerve cell that transmits electrical or chemical impulses.

neurotransmitters—chemical signals that carry nerve impulses across the synapses between neurons.

occipital lobe—the part of the cortex at the back of the head.

parietal lobe—the middle portion of the cortex at the top of the head.

Pasteur's germ theory—After proving that fermentation and decay were the work of living microscopic organisms, Louis Pasteur discovered that many diseases are caused by living pathogenic bacteria that he called germs.

penicillin—the first widely used antibiotic that halted infections by attacking pathogenic bacteria. It is produced naturally by a kind of common green bread mold.

phrenology—the elaboration of Josef Gall's original idea that brain functions were highly localized. Phrenology grew into an elaborate pseudoscience that divined human intelligence by reading bumps and dips on the head.

receptive aphasia—the inability to understand speech, usually the result of brain damage to Wernicke's area on the temporal lobe of the cortex.

seizure—a sudden, involuntary contraction of the muscles usually caused by a disruption of the normal electrical patterns of the brain. A seizure is a symptom, not a disease in itself.

sepsis—a severe bacterial infection.

spinal cord—the tract carrying the nerves from the brain stem to the rest of the body. It is protected by a flexible backbone of separate vertebrae. Animals with spinal cords, including humans, are called vertebrates.

staphylococci—a large tribe of related bacteria. They are pathogenic, meaning they cause disease, usually through wound infections or food poisoning.

streptococci—another large family of pathogenic bacteria that can infect, among other systems, the lungs and the digestive tract. When strep infects red blood cells, it can cause scarlet and rheumatic fevers.

synapse—the tiny space between the axon of one neuron and the connecting dendrite of another. Synapses are bridged by chemical messengers called neurotransmitters.

tamping iron—similar in appearance to a crowbar, a tamping iron was a specialized tool for gunpowder blasting in construction work before the invention of dynamite.

temporal lobe—the part of the cortex on the side of the head.

Resources

Damasio, Antonio. *Descartes' Error: Emotion, Reason, and the Human Brain*. New York: Grosset/Putnam, 1994. Written for a nonmedical readership, Dr. Damasio explains how our thinking about thinking has evolved. The case of Phineas Gage has a chapter all its own.

Komaroff, Anthony. *Harvard Medical School Family Health Guide*. New York: Simon & Schuster, 1999. A big medical reference book for ordinary readers, this has some nice illustrated explanations of how the brain works, plus a ton of other easily understood medical information.

Macmillan, Malcolm. *An Odd Kind of Fame: Stories of Phineas Gage*. Cambridge: MIT Press, 2000. Everything you could want to know about Phineas Gage from the world's leading authority on the case. The book also contains copies of the original medical papers by John Martyn Harlow and Henry Jacob Bigelow, plus newspaper stories from the period.

The "best place" on the Web for more information on Phineas Gage or anything else to do with brain science is "Neuroscience for Kids" (http://faculty.washington.edu/chudler/neurok.html), the brainchild of Eric Chudler, a neuroscience researcher at the University of Washington in Seattle. Dr. Chudler set up the site to provide kids with access to the latest news and information on brain science. This is a truly kid-friendly yet highly useful Web site. It even describes simple neurological experiments you can perform—for example, there's one on "handedness"—that don't involve brain surgery. It's also a great source of material and suggestions for science teachers.

Dr. Macmillan also maintains a Phineas Gage page at Deakin University in Australia at www.hbs.deakin.edu.au/gagepage/pgage.htm.

The author of this book has pretty well included everything he knows about Phineas Gage but is always interested in hearing about new developments. You can send him an e-mail message at jfleischman@ascb.org.

Index

Note: Page numbers in italics refer to photographs or illustrations.